ARKANSAS

by Domenica Di Piazza

Lerner Publications Company

You'll find this picture of yellow jasmines at the beginning of each chapter in this book. Yellow jasmines have fragrant, funnel-shaped flowers and are found in woodlands, thickets, and along roads in Arkansas. Their evergreen vines are sometimes used in the southern United States as decorations at Christmas.

Cover (left): Petit Jean Mountain in the Ouachita Mountains. Cover (right): The Ozark Mountain Hoe-Down Music Theater in Eureka Springs. Pages 2–3: Canoeing on the Buffalo River. Page 3: The Ozark Folk Festival at Mountain View.

This book is available in two editions:
Library binding by Lerner Publications Company, a division of Lerner Publishing Group
Soft cover by First Avenue Editions, an imprint of Lerner Publishing Group
241 First Avenue North
Minneapolis, MN 55401 U.S.A.

Website address: www.lernerbooks.com

Library of Congress Cataloging-in-Publication Data

Di Piazza, Domenica.
    Arkansas / by Domenica Di Piazza. (Rev. and expanded 2nd ed.)
      p.   cm. — (Hello U.S.A.)
    Includes index.
    ISBN: 0–8225–4073–8 (lib. bdg. : alk paper)
    ISBN: 0–8225–4136–X (pbk. : alk. paper)
      1. Arkansas—Juvenile literature. [1. Arkansas.] I. Title. II. Series.
    F411.3 .D5 2002
    976.7—dc21   2001000327

Manufactured in the United States of America
1 2 3 4 5 6 – JR – 07 06 05 04 03 02

CONTENTS

THE LAND

The Natural State

 HR-kuhn-saw or ahr-KAN-suhs? For many years, people disagreed about how to pronounce the name of this southern state. More than 100 years ago, Arkansas's state government decided that the official pronunciation would be AHR-kuhn-saw. With its many hot springs, sparkling lakes, and forested mountain peaks, Arkansas is a beautiful state—no matter how you say it.

Arkansas has six neighbors. To the north is Missouri. On the east, the Mississippi River separates Arkansas from the states of Tennessee and Mississippi. Louisiana borders Arkansas on the south, and Texas and Oklahoma lie to the west.

• Eureka Springs

• Yellville

Fayetteville •

Mountain View •

• Leslie

Jonesboro •

Fort Smith •

Jacksonville •

Little Rock ✪ • North Little Rock

• Scott

Helena •

Hot Springs
National Park •
• Hot Springs

Gillett •

• Murfreesboro

Pine Bluff •
Arkansas Post •

Washington •

• Rison

• Hope

Warren •

• Texarkana

• El Dorado

N
W ✦ E
S

The drawing of
Arkansas on this page is called a political map.
It shows features created by people, including
cities, railways, and parks. The map on the
facing page is called a physical map. It shows
physical features of Arkansas, such as coasts,
islands, mountains, rivers, and lakes. The colors
represent a range of elevations, or heights above
sea level (see legend box). This map also shows
the geographical regions of Arkansas.

ARKANSAS
Political Map

✪ State capital

0   20   40 Miles

0   20   40   60   80 Kilometers

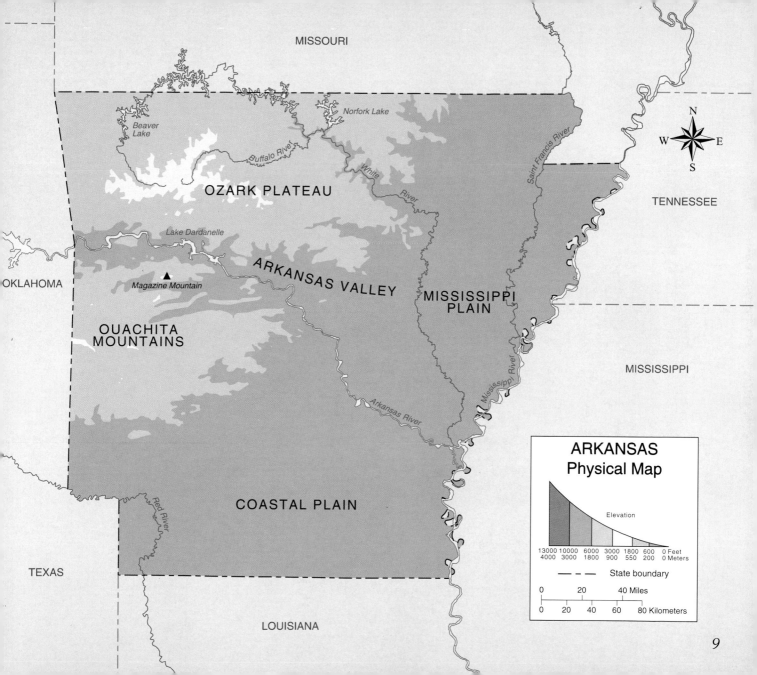

MISSOURI

Beaver Lake

Norfork Lake

Buffalo River

OZARK PLATEAU

White River

Saint Francis River

TENNESSEE

Lake Dardanelle

▲ *Magazine Mountain*

ARKANSAS VALLEY

MISSISSIPPI PLAIN

OUACHITA MOUNTAINS

MISSISSIPPI

OKLAHOMA

Arkansas River

Mississippi River

COASTAL PLAIN

Red River

TEXAS

LOUISIANA

ARKANSAS
Physical Map

Elevation

13000	10000	6000	3000	1800	600	0 Feet
4000	3000	1800	900	550	200	0 Meters

- - - State boundary

0   20   40 Miles

0   20   40   60   80 Kilometers

N
W   E
S

9

A hiker seems small beneath this massive rock archway in the mountains of western Arkansas.

The western part of Arkansas is rugged and mountainous, while the eastern and southern parts of the state are mostly flat. Northwestern land regions include the Ozark Plateau, the Arkansas Valley, and the Ouachita Mountains. The fertile soil of the Mississippi Plain covers most of eastern Arkansas. The lowlands of the Coastal Plain spread across the southwestern corner of the state.

Forests cover much of the Ozark Plateau, also known as the Ozarks. This region is part of a vast **plateau** (high flatland) that stretches across several states. Fast-running rivers have carved deep, narrow passageways called gorges between the region's limestone ridges. Farmers tend fruit orchards and raise livestock such as cattle and poultry in the Ozarks.

Along the Arkansas River in Little Rock, families compete in a fishing contest.

The Arkansas Valley is named for the Arkansas River, which winds its way southeastward to the Mississippi River. The valley is rich in underground deposits of coal and natural gas. The region also boasts the state's highest point—Magazine Mountain, which reaches 2,753 feet.

The Ouachita Mountains are well known for their underground spring-waters. People from all over the United States come to Hot Springs National Park. Here, warm water bubbles to the surface and is piped to bathhouses, where people relax in pools of the steamy water. Visitors to the region also enjoy lakes, rivers, and forested sandstone peaks.

Rice grows well in the Mississippi Plain.

Along the banks of the Mississippi River in eastern Arkansas spreads the flat land of the Mississippi Plain. Years of flooding from the Mississippi River have made the region's soil very fertile. As the floodwaters withdrew, they left behind **sediment**, or layers of sand and dirt. Land enriched by river flooding is known as a **delta**, and many Arkansans call the Mississippi Plain the Delta. Farmers in the Delta plant soybeans, rice, cotton, and wheat.

Many people earn a living from agriculture on the Coastal Plain as well. Most farmers in this region raise livestock, but some plant tomatoes, watermelons, and other fruits. Swamps and bayous, or slow-moving streams, break up the Coastal Plain's vast pine forests, which are a major source of timber. The state's largest oil wells are also found in the region.

Arkansas's chief waterways include the Mississippi, Arkansas, White, Red, and Saint Francis Rivers. Dams, which block and control the flow of water, have been built across many of Arkansas's rivers. The dams help prevent flooding by holding back water in large storage areas called reservoirs. In fact, most of Arkansas's biggest lakes are reservoirs.

A rocky ledge provides steps for a small waterfall.

The weather in Arkansas is generally warm. Summer temperatures in the south and east average about 84° F, while the mountains are usually several degrees cooler. The same is true in winter, when the average January temperature is around 45° F in the lowlands and only 39° F in the highlands of the northwest.

Every year the state receives about 49 inches of **precipitation** (rain, snow, sleet, and hail). Only about 6 inches of snow fall each year, mostly in the Ozarks and in the Ouachita Mountains.

Precipitation helps many kinds of plants grow in Arkansas. About half the land is wooded. Loblolly and shortleaf pine trees thrive in southern Arkansas. In the northwestern mountains, hardwood trees such as oaks and hickories grow alongside shortleaf pines. Cypress trees sprawl in the state's bayous and swamps.

Flowering trees in the state include magnolias, redbuds, and dogwoods. Bellflowers, yellow jasmines, and other wildflowers bloom throughout the state.

Arkansas's warm climate is ideal for magnolias *(opposite page)* and yellow jasmines *(right)*.

Arkansas's varied landscape provides homes for many wild animals. Alligators live in the state's swamps. Deer, bears, bobcats, and foxes find shelter in forests.

Night creatures called armadillos dig their underground homes in warm parts of the state. Rabbits, squirrels, opossums, muskrats, raccoons, skunks, and weasels make homes throughout Arkansas. With so much natural beauty, Arkansas lives up to its nickname—the Natural State.

An alligator *(above)* emerges from the waters of a bayou. Armadillos *(right)* came to Arkansas from the southwestern part of the United States.

THE HISTORY

From Bluff Dwellers to Little Rock

he first people to come to the area that later became Arkansas arrived at least 12,000 years ago. They were hunters who moved from place to place looking for wild game. The ancestors of American Indians, these early peoples found the region richly forested. Buffalo, deer, and bears roamed freely. Mammoths—huge elephants with giant tusks—were also plentiful.

Several thousand years later, people called bluff dwellers were making permanent homes in caves and under rock overhangs in the Ozarks. They hunted deer and wild turkeys, using darts thrown from a grooved stick. They also fished the rivers and planted corn, squash, pumpkins, and sunflowers in the rich soil along creeks.

Large earthen mounds built by early Indians are still found in parts of Arkansas. The mounds served as burial sites or as foundations of temples and homes.

Other Indians had settled near the Mississippi River by about 1000 B.C. They lived in villages and planted corn, pumpkins, and tobacco. Called mound builders, these Indians built giant earthen hills for religious ceremonies. Powerful leaders lived on top of mounds built just for them.

Indians painted images like this one on cave walls thousands of years ago. Visitors to Petit Jean State Park in northwestern Arkansas can still see these paintings.

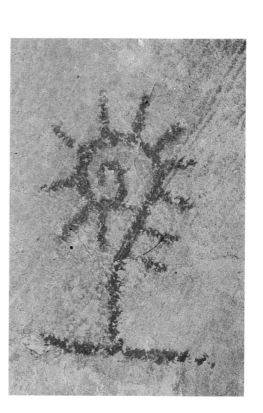

By A.D. 1500, the bluff dwellers and mound builders had disappeared. No one is quite sure why, but experts think that disease, warfare, or lack of rain may have killed many people and forced others to flee their homes.

At about the same time, in 1541, a Spanish expedition led by Hernando de Soto reached the eastern shore of the Mississippi River. The group spent nearly a month building canoes to carry the explorers, their horses, and their main food supply—a herd of pigs—across the river. For almost a year, the explorers traveled through the land that includes Arkansas, hoping to find gold. But they didn't find any riches, and by the time the group left the area, all the pigs had run off into the woods.

Spanish explorer
Hernando de Soto and
his men used captured
American Indians as
guides. De Soto was
the first European
to discover the
Mississippi River.

Groups of American Indians, some of them descended from the mound builders, were living in what later became Arkansas at the time de Soto explored the area. Members of the Caddo nations (or tribes) made tall, cone-shaped homes in villages in the southwest. For food they grew crops and hunted buffalo. To travel by river, they carved dugout canoes out of huge logs.

The Quapaw and the Osage nations eventually entered the area that later became Arkansas from the Ohio River valley far to the east. The Osage hunted throughout much of northern Arkansas. The Quapaw built rectangular, bark-covered homes in villages near the Mississippi River. They raised crops and crafted fine pottery.

Using wood and bone, the Quapaw made their own arrows and other weapons.

After de Soto's journey across what later became Arkansas, more than 100 years passed before another European set foot in the area. Looking to expand France's fur trading empire in North America, French explorers began traveling down the Mississippi River.

In 1682 French explorer René-Robert Cavelier, Sieur de La Salle, claimed the entire Mississippi River valley for France. He named the region Louisiana, after Louis XIV, the king of France. Four years later, Henri de Tonti, who had traveled with La Salle's party, returned to the Arkansas River and

What's in a Name?

Related to the Osage Indians, the Quapaw called themselves *Ugakhpa*, or "downstream people." The name refers to the fact that these Indians lived along the Mississippi River to the south of the Osage. But the Quapaw were known by early French explorers as the Arkansas Indians. This name is a combination of *arc*, a French word meaning "bow," and *ansa*, a word from the Quapaw's language meaning "people of the south wind." The state of Arkansas takes its name from the French label for the Quapaw Indians.

Until the early 1700s, when white settlers first arrived in the area, French fur traders were the most frequent visitors to Arkansas Post.

built Arkansas Post. This fur-trading site was the first permanent white settlement in Arkansas.

The French traders depended on Indians to supply furs. The Caddo, for example, traded their crops with other Indian nations in exchange for animal furs. The Caddo then gave the furs to French traders, receiving manufactured goods such as cloth, beads, and guns in return. When the French sold the furs in Europe, they made huge profits.

Few Europeans settled in Arkansas in the 1700s. Near Arkansas Post, the Arkansas River often flooded, destroying crops. So the settlers had to depend mostly on hunting and fishing for food. Every year they sent bear's oil, salted buffalo meat, and animal hides south to the growing town of New Orleans in exchange for everyday necessities.

By 1770 only 8 families, about 30 soldiers, and a handful of outlaws were living at Arkansas Post. More people came to the area after France sold Louisiana to the United States in 1803 in a deal called the Louisiana Purchase. The purchase added a vast stretch of land, including what later became Arkansas, to the United States.

Settlers from crowded states in the eastern United States flocked west to buy land, which was sold at low prices by the U.S. government. By 1819 more than 14,000 white people were living in the Arkansas area. Many settled in northern and western Arkansas, where flooding was not as big a problem as it was at Arkansas Post. That same year, the U.S. established the Territory of Arkansas.

The Arkansas Traveler

Many of the pioneers who settled in the Ozarks and in the Ouachita Mountains came from the Appalachian Mountains in the eastern United States. To their new Arkansas homes, the mountaineers brought a rich tradition of storytelling. Tales were told to pass the time around the family fireplace or at the gristmill, where farmers waited for their corn to be ground. Full of exaggeration, the stories were often set to music. One famous tale, known as "The Arkansas Traveler," was first told in the 1840s. It was adopted in 1987 as Arkansas's official state historical song.

A traveler was riding by that day
And stopped to hear him practicing away,
The cabin was afloat and his feet were wet,
But still the old man didn't seem to fret.

So the stranger said, "Now the way it seems to me,
You'd better mend your roof," said he.
But the old man said as he played away,
"I couldn't mend it now, it's a rainy day."

The traveler replied, "That's all quite true,
But this, I think, is the thing for you to do.
Get busy on a day that is fair and bright,
Then patch the old roof till it's good and tight."

But the old man kept on a-playin' his reel,
And tapped the ground with his leathery heel.
"Get along," said he, "for you give me a pain;
My cabin never leaks when it doesn't rain."

As more and more settlers came to Arkansas, the Indians' way of life changed dramatically. Most of the newcomers, for example, were farmers. They chopped down woodlands to make room for crops, and they drove away much of the wild game the Indians depended on for food. The settlers also carried diseases to which Indians had never been exposed, so many Native Americans died.

At first, the U.S. government made **treaties,** or agreements, with the Indians in Arkansas. The treaties set aside **reservations,** or areas of land for the Native Americans to live on. But the government eventually broke many of the treaties, claiming more land for settlers. In some cases, the government bought land from the Indians at low prices.

During the 1830s, the U.S. government wanted more land for white settlers. So the U.S. Army forced the Indians in Arkansas and other southeastern territories and states to move west to a place called Indian Territory in what later became Oklahoma. Many

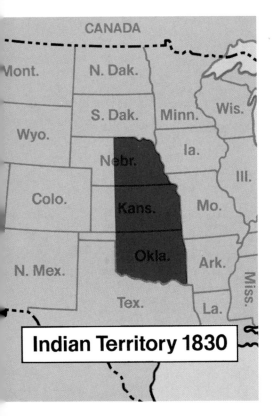

Indian Territory 1830

On plantations before the Civil War, slaves spent long days in the fields, harvesting cotton by hand.

Native Americans, forced to walk the journey, died from disease and lack of food and water. The suffering was so great that the route became known as the Trail of Tears.

By 1835 Arkansas had more than 50,000 white settlers, enough to apply for statehood. On June 15, 1836, Arkansas joined the Union as the 25th state.

Most Arkansans were farmers who worked small plots of land. But in the Mississippi and Arkansas river valleys, farmers had begun to build huge cotton **plantations.** Slaves brought to America from Africa did most of the backbreaking work of clearing the land and planting cotton on these large farms. By 1860 at least one out of four people in Arkansas was a black slave.

In the northern United States, slavery was illegal. The North tried to pressure the South to end slavery. Instead, several Southern states formed a new country, the Confederate States of America (the Confederacy). In the Confederacy, slavery was legal.

White Arkansans were split. Compared to some of its Southern neighbors, Arkansas had few slaves. Most of these slaves worked on plantations in the southern and eastern parts of the state, where many people wanted Arkansas to join the Confederacy. But farmers in northwestern Arkansas didn't depend on slave labor to make a profit and wanted the state to stay in the Union.

Jefferson county, June 9, 1851.   6—5w.

Runaway Negro in Jail.

WAS committed to th Jail of Saline coun ty, as a runaway, on th 8th day of June, 1851, negro man, who says hi name is JOHN, and tha he belongs to *Henry John* son, of Desha county, Ark He is aged about 24 or 2 years, straight in stature, quick spoken, looks ver fierce out of his eyes, and plays on the fiddle. Ha on, when apprehended, white cotton pants, coars cotton shirt, and black hat. The owner is hereb notified to come forward, prove property, and pa the expenses of committal and advertisemen otherwise the said negro will be dealt with accor ing to law.   THOMAS PACK, *Sheriff and Jailor of Saline county.* *Benton, June* 21, 1851.   7—26w.

Pay up! Pay up!!

ALL persons indebted to the undersigne whose notes and accounts are *now due*, a requested to call and *pay up*, by the 1st day of J ly next.   JOHN D. ADAMS. *June* 13, 1851.   5—

Slave owners considered their slaves to be property. Slaves who ran away could be beaten or put in jail.

Split in Two

Arkansas joined the Confederate States of America in 1861, so most Arkansans sided with the Confederacy during the Civil War. But many people in the northwestern part of the state fought for the Union. The state was officially divided after Union troops captured Little Rock—the state capital—in September 1863.

With the Union in control of the state's capital city, Arkansas's Confederate government moved its headquarters to Washington, Arkansas, in the southwestern part of the state. For the rest of the war, Arkansas had two capitals and two governors, one representing the Union and the other the Confederacy.

During the Civil War, the American flag had 35 stars—one for each state, including the states that broke away to form the Confederacy.

Although never the official Confederate flag, this battle flag is the most common symbol of the Confederacy. Arkansas still celebrates Confederate Flag Day every year on the day before Easter.

Arkansans were forced to choose sides after the Civil War broke out between the North and the South in April 1861. Most of Arkansas's soldiers, about 66,000, fought for the Confederacy. Nearly 15,000 men from northwestern Arkansas, both white and black soldiers, fought for the Union.

During the Civil War, many Arkansans lost their homes and jobs. In 1865, after four years of battle, the Confederacy admitted defeat. Southerners began to rebuild their homes and farms during a difficult postwar period called **Reconstruction.**

During this time, U.S. troops from the North moved into Arkansas to oversee the rebuilding of the state. To rejoin the Union, Arkansas had to make slavery illegal and had to allow black men to vote. In 1868 the state was readmitted.

By the late 1800s, after Reconstruction, Arkansas's government had passed a series of new laws making it

Soldiers from the Union army watch over ammunition and weapons stored at Little Rock.

almost impossible for African American men to vote. Black people also were barred from eating at the same restaurants as white people and from going to the same schools, theaters, and hotels.

In the late 1800s, industry in Arkansas progressed rapidly. Timber companies from northern states, where large forests had already been cut down, headed for Arkansas to log the state's pine forests. Arkansas made money mining bauxite (an ore from which aluminum is made) after it was discovered near Little Rock in 1887. Railroad companies built tracks across the state, and trains carried Arkansas's lumber and mineral products to market. Coal mined in western and southern Arkansas fueled the new trains.

After railroads were built in Arkansas, trains hauled logs and other goods.

Logs from Arkansas's forests arrive at a sawmill.

To make more money, railroad companies encouraged people from the East Coast and Europe to settle along Arkansas's new railways. The companies knew that people living near train stations would buy tickets to travel on the railroads and would pay to ship goods to market. Newcomers arrived from eastern states, and **immigrants** came from France, Italy, and Greece. By 1900 Arkansas's population had grown to more than 1 million people.

Hell on the Border

One of Arkansas's most famous citizens was Isaac Charles Parker, a judge at Fort Smith, Arkansas, from 1875 until 1896. Lying on Arkansas's westernmost boundary, Fort Smith bordered what remained of Indian Territory. Laws in the territory applied only to Native Americans. Bank robbers, bandits, and murderers hoped to make it to the territory to escape the law. On their way, the criminals passed through Fort Smith, giving the town a reputation as a rough place with little law and order.

But Judge Parker, who had control over western Arkansas and Indian Territory, quickly put that idea to rest. When he first arrived in Fort Smith, eighteen murderers were awaiting court trials. Of those eighteen, Parker sentenced eight to death by hanging, and one other was shot as he tried to escape. In Parker's twenty-one-year courtroom career, he sentenced more than 160 men to death, of whom about eighty were actually hanged. Outlaws called Parker the Hanging Judge, and Fort Smith gained a new reputation as Hell on the Border.

When the Arkansas River flooded in the spring of 1927, residents of Little Rock had to use boats to get around town.

Arkansas's economy continued to grow in the early 1900s. Natural gas was discovered near Fort Smith in 1901. Twenty years later, oil was drilled for the first time in Arkansas, near El Dorado. More forests were cleared in the Delta, and farmers planted fields of cotton, rice, and soybeans across the newly opened land.

Bad weather and a drop in cotton prices meant hard times for many farmers in Arkansas during the 1920s. Floods in 1927 drowned livestock and destroyed millions of acres of cropland in the Arkansas and Mississippi river valleys. Just three years later, a terrible drought hit Arkansas. Without enough water, crops withered and died.

The Great Depression of the 1930s affected people across the nation. Banks failed, businesses closed, and workers lost their jobs. Prices for cotton dropped so low that many farmers in Arkansas's Delta region couldn't afford to buy enough food to feed their families.

Arkansas's economy began to recover after the United States entered World War II in 1941. Weapons factories opened in Pine Bluff and Jacksonville. Bauxite mining increased in the state because aluminum was needed to make airplanes for the war. And the U.S. military bought Arkansas's oil to fuel airplanes and tanks.

During World War II, Arkansas provided aluminum and fuel for airplanes such as this B-17.

After the war ended in 1945, African Americans across the nation continued to work toward equality. Little Rock became a battleground in this struggle for equal rights, which was known as the **civil rights movement.**

In 1954 the U.S. Supreme Court ruled that it was illegal to prevent black students from attending the same public schools as white students. Three years later, nine African Americans registered for class at Little Rock's all-white Central High School.

Arkansas's governor, Orval Faubus, was against blacks and whites going to school together. President Dwight D. Eisenhower sent U.S. troops to Little Rock to make sure the black students were allowed to attend classes. Over time, other public facilities in Arkansas opened their doors to both blacks and whites.

By the 1960s, for the first time in the state's history, more Arkansans were earning money from manufacturing jobs than from farming. New industries came to the state, hiring workers to make everything from bicycles to doors.

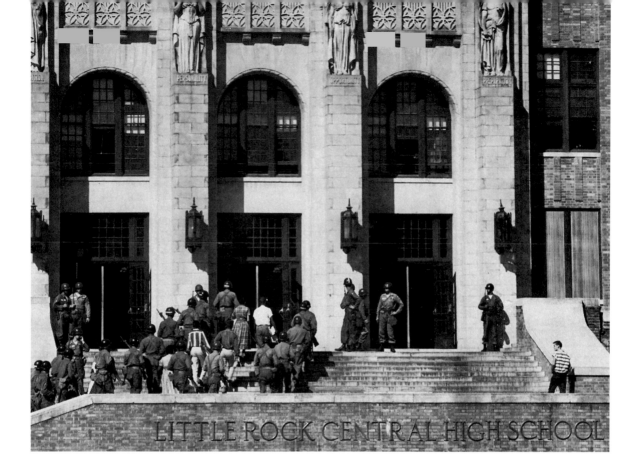

LITTLE ROCK CENTRAL HIGH SCHOOL

To help manufacturers get their products to market, Arkansas began a new transportation project. Workers deepened parts of the Arkansas River and built **locks** and dams, so big oceangoing ships could travel the river. The McClellan-Kerr Arkansas River Navigation System was completed in 1971.

U.S. government troops escorted African American students into Central High School in Little Rock in the fall of 1957.

Bill Clinton, former governor of Arkansas, and his wife, Hillary, campaigned for president in Bill's home state in 1992.

In the 1980s, under Governor Bill Clinton, many new businesses came to Arkansas and public education improved. The state bought more computers for classrooms and expanded science programs at the University of Arkansas. Clinton was elected U.S. president in 1992 and served until 2001.

The quality of life in Arkansas continues to get better. Arkansans are working to raise standards for children's education and health and to lower taxes for families. These efforts and others help ensure that Arkansans will have the opportunities and skills they need for the future.

PEOPLE & ECONOMY

Work and Play the Ozark Way

 British traveler named Charles Daubeny toured Arkansas in 1837 and wrote that the only unfriendly treatment he met while in the state was from the dogs.

At that time, about 50,000 people lived in Arkansas. The state's population has since grown to 2.7 million. That's more than 50 times as many Arkansans as when Daubeny visited the state!

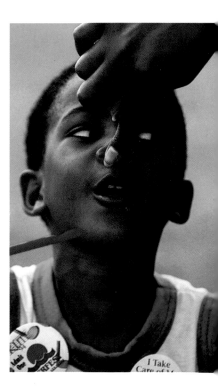

A young Arkansan hams it up at Little Rock's Riverfest, a festival held along the Arkansas River every Memorial Day weekend.

A rock climber hangs from a cliff in the Ozark Plateau.

About four out of five Arkansans (nearly 79 percent) are white people with European ancestors. Almost 16 percent of the state's residents are African Americans. Together, Asian Americans, Native Americans, and Latinos make up less than 5 percent of the state's population.

The state capitol building in Little Rock looks just like the United States Capitol in Washington, D.C.— except that it's one-fourth as big.

More than half of Arkansas's residents live in urban areas, or cities and towns. The state's largest cities are its capital—Little Rock—followed by Fort Smith, North Little Rock, Fayetteville, Jonesboro, and Pine Bluff.

Many Arkansans have jobs in these cities. More than half of all working Arkansans have service jobs, helping people or businesses. Some service workers in Arkansas teach, sell cars and homes, or drive buses and delivery trucks.

Service workers in Arkansas also ring up sales at Wal-Mart, one of the nation's largest discount stores, or stock the shelves at Dillard's—a department store known throughout the

Arkansas's government workers include sheriffs and other law-enforcement officers.

South. Both of these successful businesses have their headquarters in Arkansas.

The government employs about 14 percent of the workers in Arkansas. Some of these people work for the U.S. government at Little Rock Air Force Base, one of the largest military bases in the state.

Some of the products on store shelves are made in Arkansas. In fact, one out of every five working Arkansans has a manufacturing job. Some workers process foods such as meats, rice, soft drinks, milk, canned vegetables, and feed for farm animals. Others package chicken at Tyson Foods, the world's largest producer and processor of poultry.

At factories in Arkansas, workers make metal parts for many kinds of machinery.

Arkansas produces wood products such as these giant rolls of paper *(above)* from its timber *(left).*

Workers in Arkansas also make air conditioners, electric stoves, refrigerators, lightbulbs, and televisions. Wood and paper products are manufactured from the state's rich supply of timber.

Much of Arkansas's timber is cut down in the Coastal Plain region, where the state's largest oil fields are located. Other major mineral products in Arkansas include natural gas and bromine, which is used in making many kinds of chemicals. Altogether

only about 6,000 Arkansans, less than 1 percent of the state's jobholders, earn a living from mining.

In the 1800s, most people in Arkansas worked on farms. This is no longer true. Only about 1 in 16 employed Arkansans has a job in agriculture. Most raise livestock such as beef and dairy cattle, turkeys, hogs, and broilers (young chickens).

Farmers in Arkansas also plant rice, the state's most valuable crop. Other major crops include soybeans, cotton, hay, corn, and wheat. Grapes, peaches, tomatoes, and pecans are grown in the state as well.

About 44,000 farms are in Arkansas. Many farmers raise cattle.

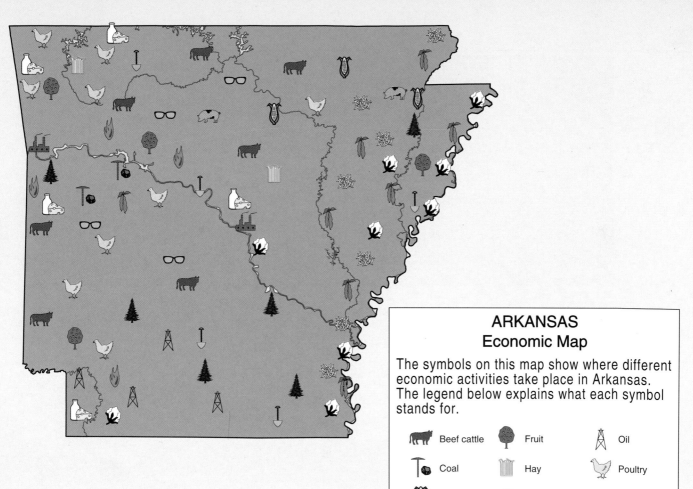

ARKANSAS
Economic Map

The symbols on this map show where different economic activities take place in Arkansas. The legend below explains what each symbol stands for.

	Beef cattle		Fruit		Oil
	Coal		Hay		Poultry
	Corn		Hogs		Rice
	Cotton		Manufacturing		Sand and gravel
	Dairy products		Natural gas		Soybeans
	Forest products		Oats		Tourism

Arkansas ranks among the top five states in raising catfish *(left)* and growing cotton *(below)*.

Arkansas's agricultural bounty makes for good eating. Cooks prepare southern specialties such as deep-fried catfish, fried chicken, cheesy grits, corn bread, and pecan pie. In between meals, there's a lot to see and do in Arkansas.

Outdoor enthusiasts in Arkansas have 51 state parks and 3 national forests to choose from. Tourists explore underground caves at Blanchard Springs Caverns in the Ozark National Forest. Backpackers hike rugged mountain trails in the Ouachita National Forest.

Adventuresome canoeists tackle the rapids on the Buffalo National River in northwestern Arkansas. Along the way, boaters pass spectacular waterfalls, towering bluffs where ancient Indians once lived, and sometimes even an armadillo or two.

History buffs can tour Toltec Mounds State Park near Little Rock to see and learn about ancient Indian mounds. The capital city's Quapaw Quarter features elegant historic homes. Students of the Civil War can visit Pea Ridge National Military Park in north-

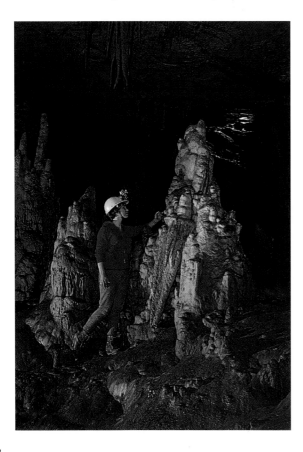

At a cave near Harrison, Arkansas, a visitor inspects underground mineral deposits.

Canoeists pass through a calm stretch of the Buffalo National River.

western Arkansas, where one of the state's most important battles took place in 1862.

Travelers on the Great River Road, a network of highways following the Mississippi River, pass through the port town of Helena. Here, visitors to the Delta Cultural Center learn about the history, art, and culture of the people in the Mississippi River valley. Many people drive south of Gillett to tour Arkansas Post National Memorial, the site of the state's earliest European settlement.

Both young and old Arkansans help the arts flourish in their state. Children paint a craft project in Little Rock *(above)*, and a banjo player performs in the Ozarks *(opposite page)*.

Across the state in Mountain View, young artists can learn to make dolls out of apples or to square dance at the Ozark Folk Center. At the nearby Ozark Heritage Arts Center in Leslie, audiences listen to Ozark storytellers and view the work of local artists. In this way, Ozark traditions are preserved and passed on to new generations.

Arkansans of all backgrounds celebrate a rich musical heritage. The state's musicians offer gospel, blues, classical, jazz, and country music. World-famous blues musicians perform at the King Biscuit Blues Festival in Helena each October. Eureka Springs hosts an annual Blues Festival in June, welcoming blues and gospel artists from all over the country. And in April, Mountain View's yearly Arkansas Folk Festival offers lively concerts of toe-tapping tunes.

Besides enjoying music, Arkansans are also enthusiastic about sports. Basketball fans fill the bleachers to watch the University of Arkansas Razorbacks play basketball. And if you hear someone hollering "Wooooo Pig SOOie!" you're sure to be at a Razorback football game. Many of the team's loyal fans wear red hats in the shape of a razorback hog and cheer for their team with this spirited hog call.

Farm Waste and Clean Water

Arkansas raises more broiler chickens than almost any other state in the country. The poultry industry in Arkansas thrives, as more Americans choose low-fat chicken over beef and pork. But while the industry provides Arkansans with jobs and money, it also pollutes the state's water resources.

Every year Arkansas's broilers produce millions of tons of manure, also known as litter, which poultry farmers must get rid of. The chicken litter contains bacteria, or germs that can cause disease. But the litter also contains chemical nutrients, or food, such as nitrogen and phosphorus. These nutrients help grasses and other plants grow. For this reason, poultry farmers use the litter to fertilize pastures where cattle graze.

Baby chicks *(left)* are raised in large chicken coops *(below)*. As the chickens grow *(opposite page)*, they produce tons of manure.

Chicken litter is used as fertilizer for Arkansas's farmland *(right)*. Rain carries the extra fertilizer into nearby rivers and lakes. Large amounts of fertilizer can cause algae to grow, which can be harmful to a waterway and the life-forms that inhabit it *(below)*.

Turkeys, another type of poultry, are raised on Arkansas farms.

Over the years, so much chicken litter has been spread on the land that it can no longer absorb all the fertilizer. When rain falls, the excess litter is carried into nearby streams, rivers, and lakes. There, the nutrients in the litter cause algae, plants that live just under the water's surface, to grow very thick.

Too much algae reduce the amount of oxygen in a lake or river. Water naturally contains oxygen, which underwater plants and animals need to live. When the algae die, tiny organisms (life-forms) in the water eat the dead algae and use up a lot of oxygen. The more algae and organisms in the water, the less oxygen fish have to breathe. As a result, fish leave the lake or stream, become sick, or die.

In addition, these waterways feed **aquifers,** or natural underground storehouses of water, from which many Arkansans take their drinking water. As the poultry industry has grown, the amount of nitrogen and bacteria has risen in aquifers near poultry farms.

Although people need a small amount of nitrogen in their diet, too much nitrogen can be poisonous. If the amount of nitrogen and disease-carrying bacteria in Arkansas's aquifers continues to increase, this water supply may become unsafe for people to drink.

To protect Arkansas's waterways and aquifers, farmers are working with the government and poultry companies in the state to come up with ways to dispose of chicken litter safely. Instead of spreading chicken litter directly onto their pastures as before, poultry farmers are encouraged to collect the litter in covered containers, where it can decay thoroughly. This process, called composting, kills harmful bacteria and reduces the amount of nitrogen in the litter.

The composted litter makes a fertilizer that is less polluting. The fertilizer that Arkansas's poultry farmers don't need for themselves can be sold to farmers in other parts of the state and across the country.

In addition, scientists are researching ways to convert chicken litter into fuel. The fuel from chicken litter could be used to provide electricity for poultry plants.

Many Arkansans agree that education is an important part of solving their water pollution problems. The state runs education programs for farmers, and another program teaches young Arkansans about water quality. Using instructions and equipment provided by the Arkansas Water Education Team (WET), junior high and high school students study a waterway in their community over a five-year period.

The ground soaks up water from rivers, streams, and lakes, filling up aquifers.

Arkansans are working together to protect the water resources in their state.

Through the WET program, students learn how to test water for signs of nutrients, bacteria, and other forms of pollution. If they find that their stream is polluted, students report it to WET and the Arkansas Department of Environmental Quality (ADEQ), which then try to discover the source of the pollution. In this way, young people are joining farmers and other Arkansans in the effort to protect Arkansas's water resources for future generations.

ALL ABOUT ARKANSAS

Fun Facts

Crater of Diamonds State Park near Murfreesboro, Arkansas, is the only place in the world where visitors can dig for diamonds and keep what they find.

The city of Texarkana belongs to Arkansas—and to Texas. Many people have their picture taken in front of the city's post office, which straddles the state line.

HOPE

HOME of the WORLD'S LARGEST WATERMELONS

Hot Springs National Park in western Arkansas was once a sacred bathing site for Native Americans. They called the region Valley of the Vapors because of the steam that rises off the pools of naturally hot springwater.

Little Rock, Arkansas's capital, was named for a small rock formation on the south side of the Arkansas River. French explorer Bernard de la Harpe chose the name in 1722 to set the settlement apart from a nearby village identified by a larger rocky ridge.

Farmers in Hope, Arkansas, grow some of the world's biggest watermelons. One weighed 262 pounds!

STATE SONG

Arkansas has four state songs, all adopted in 1987. Two are known as official state songs, and another is known as the official state historical song. "Arkansas," by Eva Ware Barnett, is the state's official anthem.

ARKANSAS

Words and music by Eva Ware Barnett

I am think-ing to-night of the South-land, Of the home of my child-hood days, Where I roamed through the woods and the mea-dows, By the mill and the brook that plays; Where the roses are in bloom, And the sweet mag-nol-ia too, Where the jas-mine is white, And the fields are vio-let blue, There a wel - come a-waits all her chil - dren Who have wan - dered a-far from home.

Chorus

Ark - an - sas, Ark - an-sas, 'Tis a name dear, 'Tis the place I call "Home, Sweet Home;" Ark - an-sas Ark - an-sas, I sa - lute thee, From thy shel - ter no more I'll roam.

AN ARKANSAS RECIPE

The town of Hope, Arkansas, where President Bill Clinton was born, is also the home of giant watermelons. Some of the watermelons grown in Hope have weighed over 200 pounds. Every August, Hope welcomes more than 40,000 visitors to its Watermelon Festival, where people eat watermelons galore. You can drink watermelon with this special lemonade, perfect for a hot Arkansas summer day.

WATERMELON LEMONADE

You will need:

6 cups watermelon, seeded and cut into cubes
¼ cup raspberries
1 cup water
⅓ cup sugar
½ cup lemon juice

1. Mix watermelon, raspberries, and water in a blender until they are smooth and liquid.
2. Strain through a fine mesh strainer into a pitcher.
3. Stir in sugar and lemon juice until sugar is dissolved.
4. Refrigerate until cold, or serve immediately over ice cubes.

HISTORICAL TIMELINE

10,000 B.C. People arrive in the area that later became Arkansas.

1000 B.C. Mound builders live in villages along the Mississippi River.

A.D. 1500 Mound builders and bluff dwellers have disappeared.

1541 Hernando de Soto explores Arkansas.

1682 René-Robert Cavelier, Sieur de La Salle, claims the Mississippi Valley, including Arkansas, for France, and calls the area Louisiana.

1686 Henri de Tonti establishes Arkansas Post.

1770 The population at Arkansas Post includes only eight families.

1803 The United States buys the Louisiana Territory, which includes the area that later became Arkansas, from France.

1819 The U.S. government establishes the Territory of Arkansas.

1836 Arkansas becomes the 25th state.

1861 Arkansas leaves the Union and joins the Confederate States of America.

1863 Union troops capture Little Rock during the Civil War.

1868 Arkansas is readmitted to the Union.

1900 The population of Arkansas reaches more than 1 million people.

1901 Natural gas is discovered near Fort Smith.

1921 Oil is drilled in Arkansas for the first time.

1927 Floods drown livestock and destroy crops.

1957 U.S. government troops escort the first African American students into Little Rock's Central High School.

1971 McClellan-Kerr Arkansas River Navigation System is completed.

1992 Former Arkansas governor Bill Clinton is elected to serve the first of two terms as the 42nd president of the United States.

1996 Governor Jim Guy Tucker resigns after being convicted of fraud involving illegal land deals.

OUTSTANDING ARKANSANS

Maya Angelou

Maya Angelou (born 1928) is a poet and author who spent much of her childhood in Stamps, Arkansas. Her most famous book is *I Know Why the Caged Bird Sings*, which tells of her years growing up in the rural South. At Bill Clinton's 1993 presidential inauguration, Angelou read a poem she had been asked to compose for the event.

Dee Alexander Brown

Dee Alexander Brown (born 1908) is a writer and historian. His best-selling book, *Bury My Heart at Wounded Knee*, describes the settlement of the western United States from the viewpoint of American Indians. Brown grew up in Stephens and Little Rock.

Helen Gurley Brown (born 1922) is an author from Green Forest, Arkansas. From 1965 until 1997, she was the editor in chief of *Cosmopolitan* magazine. Under Brown's leadership, the magazine increased in popularity and sales.

Hattie Caraway

Hattie Caraway (1878–1950) was the first woman to be elected to the U.S. Senate. She and her husband moved to Jonesboro, Arkansas, in 1902. When he died in 1931, she was appointed to finish his term in the U.S. Senate. Elected in her own right in 1932, Caraway represented Arkansas in the Senate until 1945.

Johnny Cash

Johnny Cash (born 1932) is a country-music legend from Kingsland, Arkansas. A singer, songwriter, and guitarist, Cash is best known for his recordings *I Walk the Line* and *At Folsom Prison*. In 1980 Cash was named to the Country Music Hall of Fame.

Bill Clinton (born 1946), elected to the presidency of the United States in 1992 and in 1996, is from Hope, Arkansas. Before becoming president, Clinton served for 12 years as Arkansas's governor.

Bill Clinton

Jay Hanna ("Dizzy") Dean (1911–1974), from Lucas, Arkansas, was one of the greatest pitchers in baseball history. During his career, Dean played for the Saint Louis Cardinals and the Chicago Cubs. In 1934 he won 30 games—a record that wasn't broken for 34 years. Dean was elected to the National Baseball Hall of Fame in 1953.

Dizzy Dean

Al Green (born 1946) is a musician who began performing gospel songs with his brothers when he was only nine. As an adult, Green's mix of gospel, pop, and soul has earned him fame and many hit songs, including "Tired of Being Alone" and "Let's Stay Together." Green is from Forrest City, Arkansas.

John Grisham (born 1955) is a writer from Jonesboro. He started his career as a lawyer, and the practice of law is the theme of many of his books. He is the best-selling author of *The Firm*, *The Pelican Brief*, *The Client*, *The Chamber*, and other books. Some of his books have been made into successful movies.

John Grisham

John H. Johnson (born 1918) founded Johnson Publishing Company in the 1940s. Now the largest black-owned publishing company in the world, the firm produces books and magazines, including *Ebony* and *Jet*. President Bill Clinton awarded him the Medal of Freedom in 1996. Johnson was born in Arkansas City.

John H. Johnson

Alan Ladd

Douglas MacArthur

Sidney Moncrief

Scottie Pippen

Alan Ladd (1913–1964) was one of the most popular actors of the 1940s. Born in Hot Springs, Arkansas, he was known for playing soft-spoken tough guys. Ladd's films include *This Gun for Hire* and *Shane*.

General Douglas MacArthur (1880–1964) was born in Little Rock, Arkansas. He led United States military activities in the Pacific during World War II. As supreme commander of the Allied Forces, he headed the occupation of Japan after the war. He also directed United Nations forces defending South Korea during the Korean War.

Sidney Moncrief (born 1957) was a guard for the Milwaukee Bucks basketball team in the 1980s. He was twice named the National Basketball Association (NBA) Defensive Player of the Year and was an NBA All-Star player five times during his career. Moncrief is from Little Rock.

Scottie Pippen (born 1965) is from Hamburg, Arkansas, and played college basketball at the University of Central Arkansas in Conway. He played for the Chicago Bulls for 11 seasons. During that time, he helped lead the team to win six NBA championships. He has won two Olympic gold medals. In 1996, he was selected as one of the 50 greatest players in NBA history.

Dick Powell (1904–1963) was born in Mountain View. The singer and actor starred in musical movies like *42nd Street*, but he also played a tough guy in *Murder, My Sweet* and other films. Later in his career he directed and produced movies and worked on television shows.

Brooks Robinson (born 1937) played third base for the Baltimore Orioles from 1955 to 1977. He won the Gold Glove award 16 times and was named the American League's Most Valuable Player in 1964. The Little Rock native was elected to the National Baseball Hall of Fame in 1983.

Brooks Robinson

Mary Steenburgen (born 1953), an actress, was born in Newport, Arkansas, and grew up in North Little Rock, Arkansas. Steenburgen has appeared in many motion pictures including *Back to the Future III, Parenthood,* and *Melvin and Howard,* for which she won an Academy Award in 1980.

Mary Steenburgen

William Grant Still (1895–1978), a violinist and composer, grew up in Little Rock. In 1931 Still became the first African American composer to have his work performed by a major orchestra, the Rochester Philharmonic. For this and other musical firsts, Still is known as the Dean of Afro-American Composers.

William Grant Still

Conway Twitty (1933–1993) spent part of his childhood in Helena. The country signer, also known as Harold Lloyd Jenkins, took his name from Conway, Arkansas, and Twitty, Texas. He had 55 number-one singles and is known for songs such as "Linda on My Mind," "Hello Darlin'," and "Tight Fittin' Jeans."

Sam Walton (1918–1992) was once called the richest man in America. In 1950 he moved to Arkansas from Des Moines, Iowa, and in 1962 he opened the first Wal-Mart store in Rogers, Arkansas. The giant retail company now has more than 2,400 locations in the United States and over $137 billion in yearly sales.

Sam Walton

FACTS-AT-A-GLANCE

Nicknames: Land of Opportunity, Natural State

Songs: "Arkansas (You Run Deep in Me)," "Oh, Arkansas," "The Arkansas Traveler," and "Arkansas"

Motto: *Regnat Populus* (The People Rule)

Flower: apple blossom

Tree: pine

Bird: mockingbird

Mammal: white-tailed deer

Fish: largemouth bass

Insect: honeybee

Gem: diamond

Date and ranking of statehood: June 15, 1836, the 25th state

Capital: Little Rock

Area: 52,075 square miles

Rank in area, nationwide: 27th

Average January temperature: 40° F

Average July temperature: 81° F

Centered on Arkansas's state flag is a large white diamond. It represents a mine in Murfreesboro, Arkansas—the only diamond mine known to exist in the United States. The 25 white stars show that Arkansas was the 25th state to join the Union.

POPULATION GROWTH

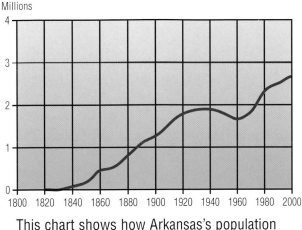

Millions

This chart shows how Arkansas's population has grown from 1820 to 2000.

The state seal of Arkansas was adopted in 1907. It shows symbols of industry and agriculture along with an American eagle. Above the eagle is the Goddess of Liberty and on either side stand the Angel of Mercy and the Sword of Liberty.

Population: 2,673,400 (2000 census)

Rank in population, nationwide: 33rd

Major cities and populations: (2000 census) Little Rock (183,133), Fort Smith (80,268), North Little Rock (60,433), Fayetteville (58,047)

U.S. senators: 2

U.S. representatives: 4

Electoral votes: 6

Natural resources: bauxite, bromine, coal, fertile soil, forests, gemstones, granite, gypsum, limestone, marble, natural gas, petroleum, sand and gravel

Agricultural products: beef cattle, broiler chickens, catfish, corn, cotton, eggs, grain sorghum, hay, hogs, milk, rice, soybeans, turkeys, wheat

Manufactured goods: air conditioners, animal feed, canned vegetables, cardboard, electric ranges, light bulbs, paper bags, refrigerators, soft drinks, televisions, tissues

WHERE ARKANSANS WORK

Services—56 percent (services include jobs in trade; community, social, and personal services; finance, insurance, and real estate; transportation, communication, and utilities)

Manufacturing—18 percent

Government—14 percent

Agriculture—6 percent

Construction—6 percent

Mining—less than .5 percent

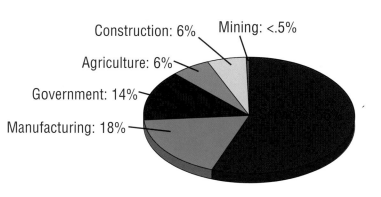

Construction: 6% Mining: <.5%
Agriculture: 6%
Government: 14%
Manufacturing: 18%

GROSS STATE PRODUCT

Services—53 percent

Manufacturing—24 percent

Government—12 percent

Agriculture—6 percent

Construction—4 percent

Mining—1 percent

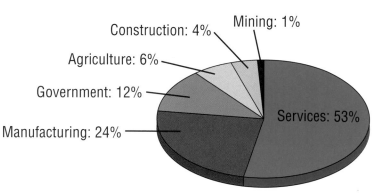

Construction: 4% Mining: 1%
Agriculture: 6%
Government: 12%
Manufacturing: 24%
Services: 53%

STATE WILDLIFE

Mammals: armadillo, black bear, bobcat, deer, fox, mink, muskrat, opossum, rabbit, raccoon, skunk, squirrel, weasel, woodchuck

Birds: blue jay, brown-headed nuthatch, brown thrasher, cardinal, goldfinch, mockingbird, painted bunting, pheasant, phoebe, quail, robin, warbler, whippoorwill, wild duck, wild goose, wild turkey, woodcock

Fish: bass, bream, catfish, crappie, drum, perch, pickerel, sturgeon, trout

Reptiles and amphibians: blue racer, copperhead, coral snake, frog, garter snake, king snake, lizard, rattlesnake, turtle, water moccasin

Wild plants: American bellflower, ferns, herbs, orchid, passionflower, water lily, wild verbena, yellow jasmine

Trees: ash, basswood, buckeye, dogwood, elm, hackberry, hawthorn, hickory, holly, locust, magnolia, maple, oak, plum, redbud, red haw, wild cherry, willow

Red fox

PLACES TO VISIT

Arkansas Arts Center, Little Rock
Located in MacArthur Park, the center houses galleries in which drawings, paintings, and sculptures from the 1500s to the present are displayed. The center is also the home of the Arkansas Children's Theatre.

Arkansas Post National Memorial, near Gillett
This is the site of the first permanent European settlement in Arkansas. Arkansas Post also served as the first territorial capital of Arkansas and was the site of a Civil War battle. The memorial features a wildlife sanctuary and a museum explaining the site's history.

Buffalo National River, northwestern Arkansas
The country's first national river winds through the Ozarks and into the White River. As hikers and canoeists travel down the river, they can see high bluffs, waterfalls, caves, and diverse plant life and wildlife.

Crater of Diamonds State Park, near Murfreesboro
At the only active diamond mine in North America, visitors can search for diamonds and keep what they find. More than 70,000 diamonds have been found here since 1906.

Eureka Springs, northwest Ozarks
This resort town was built in the late 1800s and features art galleries, gardens, museums, and a steam-powered train.

Fort Smith National Historic Site, Fort Smith

One of the first U.S. military posts in the Louisiana Territory is open to the public. Visitors can see Judge Isaac C. Parker's courtroom, jail, and the gallows where criminals were hanged.

Hot Springs National Park, west central Arkansas

The country's oldest national park protects 47 natural hot springs. People once visited the hot springs and the bathhouses on Bathhouse Row to improve their health. Tourists can bathe in the hot springs, hike, camp, and picnic in the park.

Ozark Folk Center, Mountain View

Pioneer skills and lifestyles are preserved at this living museum. Visitors of all ages can attend folk music concerts and learn traditional arts, crafts, and trades.

Ozark National Forest, northwestern Arkansas

This large wilderness area, located in the mountains of northwestern Arkansas, offers hiking, mountain biking, horseback riding, and camping. One of the main attractions is the Blanchard Springs Caverns near Mountain View, with its spectacular rock formations and large underground chambers.

Pioneer Village, Rison

This re-creation of an 1800s village features a doctor's home, a general store, a blacksmith shop, a church, and a post office.

Toltec Mounds State Park, Scott

The largest Native American mounds in Arkansas are the remains of a large ceremonial and governmental complex built by the people of the Plum Bayou Culture over 1,200 years ago.

The bathhouses along Bathhouse Row at Hot Springs National Park

ANNUAL EVENTS

Arkansas Folk Festival, Mountain View—*April*

Magnolia Blossom Festival and World Championship Steak Cook-Off, Magnolia—*May*

Riverfest, Little Rock—*May*

Annual Blues Festival, Eureka Springs—*June*

Pink Tomato Festival, Warren—*June*

Hope Watermelon Festival, Hope—*August*

Four States Fair and Rodeo, Texarkana—*September*

King Biscuit Blues Festival, Helena—*October*

Turkey Trot Festival, Yellville—*October*

National Bluegrass Fiddle Championships, Mountain View—*November*

LEARN MORE ABOUT ARKANSAS

BOOKS

General

Fradin, Dennis Brindell, and Judith Bloom Fradin. *Arkansas.* Chicago: Children's Press, 1996.

Altman, Linda Jacobs. *Arkansas.* New York: Benchmark Books, 2000. For older readers.

Special Interest

Cwiklik, Robert. *Bill Clinton: President of the 90's.* Brookfield, CT: Millbrook, 1997. This biography tells about the former Arkansas governor's childhood and his road to the presidency.

Lucas, Eileen. *Cracking the Wall: The Struggles of the Little Rock Nine.* Minneapolis: Carolrhoda Books, 1997. This illustrated story for younger readers describes the courageous black students who broke the color barrier at Little Rock's Central High School in 1957.

O'Neill, Laurie A. *Little Rock: The Desegregation of Central High.* Brookfield, CT: Millbrook, 1994. O'Neill describes the historical and social background of the civil rights movement and the process of integrating Central High School in Little Rock.

Schnakenberg, Robert. *Scottie Pippen: Reluctant Superstar.* Minneapolis: Lerner Publications Company, 1997. Follows basketball star Scottie Pippen from his roots in small-town Arkansas to his triumphs with the Chicago Bulls.

Spain, Valerie. *Meet Maya Angelou.* New York: Random House, 1994. Chronicles the life and achievements of the multi-talented author, who spent some of her youth in Arkansas.

Fiction

Dengler, Marianna. *Fiddlin' Sam.* Flagstaff, AZ: Rising Moon, 1999. Sam travels through the Ozark Mountains playing his fiddle, to the delight of both young and old. As he grows older, he searches for someone to carry on his fiddling after he's gone.

Hersenhorn, Esther. *There Goes Lowell's Party!* New York: Holiday House, 1998. This brightly colored picture book is set in the Ozarks. Young Lowell's birthday party is threatened by rain, but he hopes his resourceful family will get there no matter what.

WEBSITES

Arkansas State Government
<http://www.state.ar.us/>
This site provides facts about Arkansas state departments, agencies, and services.

Arkansas Department of Parks and Tourism
<http://www.arkansas.com/>
The state's official tourism site offers information about activities, events, state parks, and other destinations in Arkansas.

Arkansas Online
<http://www.ardemgaz.com/>
For an update on current Arkansas events, read the electronic edition of the *Arkansas Democrat-Gazette*, the state's major daily newspaper.

Arkansas Secretary of State–Communications and Education
<http://www.sosweb.state.ar.us/about_ark/>
Find answers to your questions about Arkansas history, state symbols, and state songs.

Hot Springs National Park
<http://www.nps.gov/hosp/>
Learn more about the history of Arkansas's national park, and take a virtual tour of the park by following the "In depth" link.

PRONUNCIATION GUIDE

Arkansas (AHR-kuhn-saw)

Caddo (KAD-oh)

de Soto, Hernando (dih SOH-toh, ehr-NAHN-doh)

Fayetteville (FAY-uht-vuhl)

Harpe, Bernard de la (ahrp, behr-NAHR duh lah)

Helena (HEHL-uh-nuh)

La Salle, René-Robert Cavelier, Sieur de (luh SAL, ruh-NAY-roh-BEHR ka-vuhl-YAY, SYER duh)

Murfreesboro (MUHR-freez-buhr-uh)

Osage (oh-SAYJ)

Ouachita (WAH-shuh-taw)

Quapaw (KWAW-paw)

GLOSSARY

aquifer: an underwater layer of rock, sand, or gravel containing water that can be drawn out for use above ground

civil rights movement: a fight to gain equal rights, or freedoms, for all citizens regardless of race, religion, or sex

delta: a triangular piece of land at the mouth of a river. A delta is formed from soil deposited by the river.

immigrant: a person who moves into a foreign country and settles there

lock: an enclosed, water-filled chamber in a canal or river used to raise or lower boats beyond the site of a waterfall. Boats can enter the lock through gates at either end.

plantation: a large estate on which workers live and raise crops. In the past, plantations usually used slaves.

plateau: a large, relatively flat area that stands above the surrounding land

precipitation: rain, snow, and other forms of moisture that fall to earth

Reconstruction: the period from 1865 to 1877 during which the Southern states rejoined the Union after the Civil War. Before rejoining, a Southern state had to pass a law allowing black men to vote. Places destroyed in the war were rebuilt and industries were developed.

reservation: public land set aside by the government for Native Americans

sediment: solid materials—such as soil, sand, and minerals—that are carried into a body of water by wind, ice, or running water

treaty: an agreement, usually having to do with peace or trade

INDEX

PHOTO ACKNOWLEDGMENTS

Cover photographs by William A. Bake/CORBIS (left) and Buddy Mays/CORBIS (right); Digital Cartographics, pp. 1, 8, 9, 46; © Connie Toops pp. 2–3, 45, 51; Buddy Mays/Travel Stock, pp. 3, 17, 39, 43, 49, 61, 75; Stephen Kirkpatrick, pp. 4 (detail), 7 (detail), 14, 15, 17 (detail), 39 (detail), 47 (right), 52 (detail); © Scott T. Smith, p. 6; A.C. Haralson/Arkansas Dept. of Parks & Tourism, pp. 7, 11, 18, 50, 80; Dixie Knight, pp. 10, 19, 38, 41; Photo Source/Garry McMichael, pp. 12, 47 (left), 48, 57, 60, 79; © Terry Donnelly/Dembinsky Photo, p. 13; Diane Cooper, 16 (left), 40; *Outdoor Oklahoma*, the official publication of the Oklahoma Dept. of Wildlife Conservation, p. 16 (right); Library of Congress, pp. 20, 21; Historical Pictures relating to the Louisiana Purchase issued by the *St. Louis Globe-Democrat*, 1902, p. 23; Arkansas History Commission, p. 27; UCA Archives, pp. 28, 30, 34, 66 (top, second from top), 69 (second from bottom); Tim Seeley, pp. 29, 63, 71, 72; Arkansas State University Museum Archives, pp. 31, 32; Fort Smith National Historic Park, p. 33; Smithsonian Institution, p. 35; *Arkansas Democrat-Gazette*, p. 37; © Frank Siteman/NE Stock Photo, p. 42; Frederica Georgia, p. 44 (left); Garry D. McMichael, Root Resources, p. 44 (right); James Blank, Root Resources, p. 54 (right); USDA, pp. 52, 53 (top), 54 (left); Arkansas Dept. of Parks & Tourism, p. 53 (bottom); Jerry Hennen, p. 55; Arkansas Dept. of Parks and Tourism, p. 58; Picture Collection, Special Collections Division, University of Arkansas Libraries, Fayetteville, p. 66 (second from bottom); Hollywood Book & Poster, pp. 66 (bottom), 68 (top); Maine South High School, p. 67 (top); National Baseball Library, Cooperstown, NY, p. 67 (second from top); Globe Photos, Inc.: © Andrea Renault, p. 67 (second from bottom), © Lisa Rose, p. 69 (second from top); Johnson Publishing Co., p. 67 (bottom); MacArthur Memorial, p. 68 (second from top); Milwaukee Bucks, p. 68 (second from bottom); © Duomo/CORBIS, p. 68 (bottom); Baltimore Orioles, p. 69 (top); Wal-Mart Stores, Inc., p. 69 (bottom); Jean Matheny, p. 70 (top); © Mary Ann McDonald/CORBIS, p. 73.